The Wise Writer's

Concept Journal

CREATE PRESERVE RECALL

Anna Questerly

Published in U.S.A.

ISBN-13: 978-1723034541
ISBN-10: 1723034541

For information about having Anna Questerly speak to your group, school, conference, or workshop, send an email line to AnnaQuesterly@gmail.com with "Request for Speaking Engagement" in the subject line.

For information about special discounts on bulk purchases, send an email to AnnaQuesterly@gmail.com with "Bulk Purchases: in the subject line.

Table of Contents

Project Title	Page
1.	1
2.	5
3.	9
4.	13
5.	17
6.	21
7.	25
8.	29
9.	33
10.	37
11.	41
12.	45
13.	49
14.	53
15.	57
16.	61
17.	65

Table of Contents continued

	Project Title	Page
18.		69
19.		73
20.		77
21.		81
22.		85
23.		89
24.		93
25.		97
26.		101
27.		105
28.		109
29.		113
30.		117
31.		121
32.		125
33.		129

Table of Contents continued

	Project Title	Page
34.		133
35.		137
36.		141
37.		145
38.		149
39.		153
40.		157
41.		161
42.		165
43.		169
45.		173
46.		177
47.		181
48.		185
49.		189
50.		193

Dear Wise Writer,

As a fellow creative, I'm betting you, too, have come up with a blockbuster idea for a book and jotted it down somewhere so you could write it when you had more time. I'd also feel comfortable betting you can't find it now.

Well, maybe you can find one of them, but I feel the odds are in my favor that you can't find them all. I mean, I write my genius ideas in a journal...or a piece of scrap paper... or on that napkin at the diner... or typed that email to myself and saved it in a folder... or opened a word doc and saved it in Dropbox... or, well, you get the picture.

And I feel lucky if I'm able to find the one I'm looking for. I have a theory that after a month or two, they are sucked into the nearest black hole and spit out into another universe for a different writer to latch on to. Yes, science has proved this is where the AHA and Eureka moments come from.

I fell in love with the *Wise Writer's Workbook* I created a few months ago, but soon realized, even as the author, I could go broke using a brand new workbook for each of my ideas. I needed something else; maybe a bit smaller and able to hold more ideas, and maybe fewer details – And this, boys and girls, is how the *Wise Writer's Concept Journal* was born.

Now, once I'm finished with a novel, I can go to my *Wise Writer's Concept Journal*, choose my next idea, and start moving information over to the *Wise Writer's Workbook.* You gotta love a great system, right?

Go ahead Wise Writer – it's your journal now. Have fun filling it up. Make sure to fill in your title and page number in the fill-in-the-blank table of contents so you can easily find it when you're ready.

Don't worry if you're having trouble coming up with ideas, on page 129 you'll find some great resources to spark your creativity.

Oh, and if you think of additional features you'd like to see in a future edition, drop me a line at AnnaQuesterly@gmail.com. Your suggestion might be included next time.

Keep on writin'

P.S. If you do find the *Wise Writer's Concept Journal* helpful, I hope you will consider leaving a great review online and telling your writing friends about it. Thanks bunches!

Project Information

Working Title:

Genre/Subject:

Estimated Word Count:

Target Reader:

Setting:

Inciting Idea:

Blockbuster Premise:

Additional Notes

Character Information

Action Verb:

Name:

Synonyms for

Age: Gender: Race:

Action Verbs:

Profession:

Social Class:

Strengths/Abilities:

Fears/Dislikes:

Transportation:

History:

Goal:

Motivation:

Conflict:

Character Information

Action Verb:

Name:

Age: Gender: Race:

Profession:

Social Class:

Strengths/Abilities:

Fears/Dislikes:

Transportation:

History:

Goal:

Motivation:

Conflict:

Synonyms for Action Verbs:

Project Information

Working Title:

Genre/Subject:

Estimated Word Count:

Target Reader:

Setting:

Inciting Idea:

Blockbuster Premise:

Additional Notes

Character Information

Action Verb:

Name:

Synonyms for Action Verbs:

Age: Gender: Race:

Profession:

Social Class:

Strengths/Abilities:

Fears/Dislikes:

Transportation:

History:

Goal:

Motivation:

Conflict:

Character Information

Action Verb:

Name:

Synonyms for Action Verbs:

Age: Gender: Race:

Profession:

Social Class:

Strengths/Abilities:

Fears/Dislikes:

Transportation:

History:

Goal:

Motivation:

Conflict:

Project Information

Working Title:

Genre/Subject:

Estimated Word Count:

Target Reader:

Setting:

Inciting Idea:

Blockbuster Premise:

Additional Notes

Character Information

Action Verb:

Synonyms for Action Verbs:

Name:

Age: Gender: Race:

Profession:

Social Class:

Strengths/Abilities:

Fears/Dislikes:

Transportation:

History:

Goal:

Motivation:

Conflict:

Character Information

Action Verb:

Synonyms for Action Verbs:

Name:

Age: Gender: Race:

Profession:

Social Class:

Strengths/Abilities:

Fears/Dislikes:

Transportation:

History:

Goal:

Motivation:

Conflict:

Project Information

Working Title:

Genre/Subject:

Estimated Word Count:

Target Reader:

Setting:

Inciting Idea:

Blockbuster Premise:

Additional Notes

Character Information

Action Verb:

Name:

Age: Gender: Race:

Profession:

Social Class:

Strengths/Abilities:

Fears/Dislikes:

Transportation:

Synonyms for Action Verbs:

History:

Goal:

Motivation:

Conflict:

Character Information

Action Verb:

Name:

Synonyms for Action Verbs:

Age: Gender: Race:

Profession:

Social Class:

Strengths/Abilities:

Fears/Dislikes:

Transportation:

History:

Goal:

Motivation:

Conflict:

Project Information

Working Title:

Genre/Subject:

Estimated Word Count:

Target Reader:

Setting:

Inciting Idea:

Blockbuster Premise:

Additional Notes

Character Information

Action Verb:

Synonyms for

Action Verbs:

Name:

Age: Gender: Race:

Profession:

Social Class:

Strengths/Abilities:

Fears/Dislikes:

Transportation:

History:

Goal:

Motivation:

Conflict:

Character Information

Action Verb:

Name:

Synonyms for Action Verbs:

Age: Gender: Race:

Profession:

Social Class:

Strengths/Abilities:

Fears/Dislikes:

Transportation:

History:

Goal:

Motivation:

Conflict:

Project Information

Working Title:

Genre/Subject:

Estimated Word Count:

Target Reader:

Setting:

Inciting Idea:

Blockbuster Premise:

Additional Notes

Character Information

Action Verb:

Name:

Age: Gender: Race:

Profession:

Social Class:

Strengths/Abilities:

Fears/Dislikes:

Transportation:

Synonyms for Action Verbs:

History:

Goal:

Motivation:

Conflict:

Character Information

Action Verb:

Name:

Synonyms for Action Verbs:

Age: Gender: Race:

Profession:

Social Class:

Strengths/Abilities:

Fears/Dislikes:

Transportation:

History:

Goal:

Motivation:

Conflict:

Project Information

Working Title:

Genre/Subject:

Estimated Word Count:

Target Reader:

Setting:

Inciting Idea:

Blockbuster Premise:

Additional Notes

Character Information

Action Verb:

Name:

Synonyms for Action Verbs:

Age: Gender: Race:

Profession:

Social Class:

Strengths/Abilities:

Fears/Dislikes:

Transportation:

History:

Goal:

Motivation:

Conflict:

Character Information

Action Verb:

Name:

Synonyms for Action Verbs:

Age: Gender: Race:

Profession:

Social Class:

Strengths/Abilities:

Fears/Dislikes:

Transportation:

History:

Goal:

Motivation:

Conflict:

Project Information

Working Title:

Genre/Subject:

Estimated Word Count:

Target Reader:

Setting:

Inciting Idea:

Blockbuster Premise:

Additional Notes

Character Information

Action Verb:

Name:

Synonyms for Action Verbs:

Age: Gender: Race:

Profession:

Social Class:

Strengths/Abilities:

Fears/Dislikes:

Transportation:

History:

Goal:

Motivation:

Conflict:

Character Information

Action Verb:

Name:

Synonyms for

Age: Gender: Race:

Action Verbs:

Profession:

Social Class:

Strengths/Abilities:

Fears/Dislikes:

Transportation:

History:

Goal:

Motivation:

Conflict:

Project Information

Working Title:

Genre/Subject:

Estimated Word Count:

Target Reader:

Setting:

Inciting Idea:

Blockbuster Premise:

Additional Notes

Character Information

Action Verb:

Name:

Synonyms for Action Verbs:

Age: Gender: Race:

Profession:

Social Class:

Strengths/Abilities:

Fears/Dislikes:

Transportation:

History:

Goal:

Motivation:

Conflict:

Character Information

Action Verb:

Name:

Synonyms for

Age: Gender: Race:

Action Verbs:

Profession:

Social Class:

Strengths/Abilities:

Fears/Dislikes:

Transportation:

History:

Goal:

Motivation:

Conflict:

Additional Notes

Project Information

Working Title:

Genre/Subject:

Estimated Word Count:

Target Reader:

Setting:

Inciting Idea:

Blockbuster Premise:

Character Information

Action Verb:

Name:

Age: Gender: Race:

Profession:

Social Class:

Strengths/Abilities:

Fears/Dislikes:

Transportation:

History:

Goal:

Motivation:

Conflict:

Synonyms for Action Verbs:

Character Information

Action Verb:

Name:

Synonyms for Action Verbs:

Age: Gender: Race:

Profession:

Social Class:

Strengths/Abilities:

Fears/Dislikes:

Transportation:

History:

Goal:

Motivation:

Conflict:

Project Information

Working Title:

Genre/Subject:

Estimated Word Count:

Target Reader:

Setting:

Inciting Idea:

Blockbuster Premise:

Additional Notes

Character Information

Action Verb:

Name:

Synonyms for Action Verbs:

Age: Gender: Race:

Profession:

Social Class:

Strengths/Abilities:

Fears/Dislikes:

Transportation:

History:

Goal:

Motivation:

Conflict:

Character Information

Action Verb:

Name:

Synonyms for Action Verbs:

Age: Gender: Race:

Profession:

Social Class:

Strengths/Abilities:

Fears/Dislikes:

Transportation:

History:

Goal:

Motivation:

Conflict:

Project Information

Working Title:

Genre/Subject:

Estimated Word Count:

Target Reader:

Setting:

Inciting Idea:

Blockbuster Premise:

Additional Notes

Character Information

Action Verb:

Name:

Age: Gender: Race:

Profession:

Social Class:

Strengths/Abilities:

Fears/Dislikes:

Transportation:

Synonyms for Action Verbs:

History:

Goal:

Motivation:

Conflict:

Character Information

Action Verb:

Name:

Age: Gender: Race:

Profession:

Social Class:

Strengths/Abilities:

Fears/Dislikes:

Transportation:

History:

Goal:

Motivation:

Conflict:

Synonyms for Action Verbs:

Project Information

Working Title:

Genre/Subject:

Estimated Word Count:

Target Reader:

Setting:

Inciting Idea:

Blockbuster Premise:

Additional Notes

Character Information

Action Verb:

Name:

Synonyms for

Age: Gender: Race:

Action Verbs:

Profession:

Social Class:

Strengths/Abilities:

Fears/Dislikes:

Transportation:

History:

Goal:

Motivation:

Conflict:

Character Information

Action Verb:

Name:

Synonyms for

Age: Gender: Race:

Action Verbs:

Profession:

Social Class:

Strengths/Abilities:

Fears/Dislikes:

Transportation:

History:

Goal:

Motivation:

Conflict:

Project Information

Working Title:

Genre/Subject:

Estimated Word Count:

Target Reader:

Setting:

Inciting Idea:

Blockbuster Premise:

Additional Notes

Character Information

Action Verb:

Name:

Synonyms for Action Verbs:

Age: Gender: Race:

Profession:

Social Class:

Strengths/Abilities:

Fears/Dislikes:

Transportation:

History:

Goal:

Motivation:

Conflict:

Character Information

Action Verb:

Name:

Synonyms for Action Verbs:

Age: Gender: Race:

Profession:

Social Class:

Strengths/Abilities:

Fears/Dislikes:

Transportation:

History:

Goal:

Motivation:

Conflict:

Project Information

Working Title:

Genre/Subject:

Estimated Word Count:

Target Reader:

Setting:

Inciting Idea:

Blockbuster Premise:

Additional Notes

Character Information

Action Verb:

Name:

Synonyms for Action Verbs:

Age: Gender: Race:

Profession:

Social Class:

Strengths/Abilities:

Fears/Dislikes:

Transportation:

History:

Goal:

Motivation:

Conflict:

Character Information

Action Verb:

Name:

Synonyms for Action Verbs:

Age: Gender: Race:

Profession:

Social Class:

Strengths/Abilities:

Fears/Dislikes:

Transportation:

History:

Goal:

Motivation:

Conflict:

Project Information

Working Title:

Genre/Subject:

Estimated Word Count:

Target Reader:

Setting:

Inciting Idea:

Blockbuster Premise:

Additional Notes

Character Information

Action Verb:

Name:

Age: Gender: Race:

Profession:

Social Class:

Strengths/Abilities:

Fears/Dislikes:

Transportation:

History:

Goal:

Motivation:

Conflict:

Synonyms for Action Verbs:

Character Information

Action Verb:

Name:

Synonyms for Action Verbs:

Age: Gender: Race:

Profession:

Social Class:

Strengths/Abilities:

Fears/Dislikes:

Transportation:

History:

Goal:

Motivation:

Conflict:

Project Information

Working Title:

Genre/Subject:

Estimated Word Count:

Target Reader:

Setting:

Inciting Idea:

Blockbuster Premise:

Additional Notes

Character Information

Action Verb:

Name:

Synonyms for

Age: Gender: Race:

Action Verbs:

Profession:

Social Class:

Strengths/Abilities:

Fears/Dislikes:

Transportation:

History:

Goal:

Motivation:

Conflict:

Character Information

Action Verb:

Name:

Synonyms for Action Verbs:

Age: Gender: Race:

Profession:

Social Class:

Strengths/Abilities:

Fears/Dislikes:

Transportation:

History:

Goal:

Motivation:

Conflict:

Project Information

Working Title:

Genre/Subject:

Estimated Word Count:

Target Reader:

Setting:

Inciting Idea:

Blockbuster Premise:

Additional Notes

Character Information

Action Verb:

Name:

Synonyms for

Age: Gender: Race:

Action Verbs:

Profession:

Social Class:

Strengths/Abilities:

Fears/Dislikes:

Transportation:

History:

Goal:

Motivation:

Conflict:

Character Information

Action Verb:

Name:

Synonyms for Action Verbs:

Age: Gender: Race:

Profession:

Social Class:

Strengths/Abilities:

Fears/Dislikes:

Transportation:

History:

Goal:

Motivation:

Conflict:

Project Information

Working Title:

Genre/Subject:

Estimated Word Count:

Target Reader:

Setting:

Inciting Idea:

Blockbuster Premise:

Additional Notes

Character Information

Action Verb:

Name:

Synonyms for Action Verbs:

Age: Gender: Race:

Profession:

Social Class:

Strengths/Abilities:

Fears/Dislikes:

Transportation:

History:

Goal:

Motivation:

Conflict:

Character Information

Action Verb:

Name:

Synonyms for Action Verbs:

Age: Gender: Race:

Profession:

Social Class:

Strengths/Abilities:

Fears/Dislikes:

Transportation:

History:

Goal:

Motivation:

Conflict:

Project Information

Working Title:

Genre/Subject:

Estimated Word Count:

Target Reader:

Setting:

Inciting Idea:

Blockbuster Premise:

Additional Notes

Character Information

Action Verb:

Name:

Synonyms for Action Verbs:

Age: Gender: Race:

Profession:

Social Class:

Strengths/Abilities:

Fears/Dislikes:

Transportation:

History:

Goal:

Motivation:

Conflict:

Character Information

Action Verb:

Name:

Age: Gender: Race:

Profession:

Social Class:

Strengths/Abilities:

Fears/Dislikes:

Transportation:

History:

Goal:

Motivation:

Conflict:

Synonyms for Action Verbs:

Project Information

Working Title:

Genre/Subject:

Estimated Word Count:

Target Reader:

Setting:

Inciting Idea:

Blockbuster Premise:

Additional Notes

Character Information

Action Verb:

Name:

Synonyms for Action Verbs:

Age: Gender: Race:

Profession:

Social Class:

Strengths/Abilities:

Fears/Dislikes:

Transportation:

History:

Goal:

Motivation:

Conflict:

Character Information

Action Verb:

Synonyms for Action Verbs:

Name:

Age: Gender: Race:

Profession:

Social Class:

Strengths/Abilities:

Fears/Dislikes:

Transportation:

History:

Goal:

Motivation:

Conflict:

Project Information

Working Title:

Genre/Subject:

Estimated Word Count:

Target Reader:

Setting:

Inciting Idea:

Blockbuster Premise:

Additional Notes

Character Information

Action Verb:

Name:

Synonyms for Action Verbs:

Age: Gender: Race:

Profession:

Social Class:

Strengths/Abilities:

Fears/Dislikes:

Transportation:

History:

Goal:

Motivation:

Conflict:

Character Information

Action Verb:

Name:

Synonyms for

Age: Gender: Race:

Action Verbs:

Profession:

Social Class:

Strengths/Abilities:

Fears/Dislikes:

Transportation:

History:

Goal:

Motivation:

Conflict:

Project Information

Working Title:

Genre/Subject:

Estimated Word Count:

Target Reader:

Setting:

Inciting Idea:

Blockbuster Premise:

Additional Notes

Character Information

Action Verb:

Name:

Synonyms for Action Verbs:

Age: Gender: Race:

Profession:

Social Class:

Strengths/Abilities:

Fears/Dislikes:

Transportation:

History:

Goal:

Motivation:

Conflict:

Character Information

Action Verb:

Name:

Synonyms for Action Verbs:

Age: Gender: Race:

Profession:

Social Class:

Strengths/Abilities:

Fears/Dislikes:

Transportation:

History:

Goal:

Motivation:

Conflict:

Project Information

Working Title:

Genre/Subject:

Estimated Word Count:

Target Reader:

Setting:

Inciting Idea:

Blockbuster Premise:

Additional Notes

Character Information

Action Verb:

Name:

Synonyms for Action Verbs:

Age: Gender: Race:

Profession:

Social Class:

Strengths/Abilities:

Fears/Dislikes:

Transportation:

History:

Goal:

Motivation:

Conflict:

Character Information

Action Verb:

Name:

Synonyms for Action Verbs:

Age: Gender: Race:

Profession:

Social Class:

Strengths/Abilities:

Fears/Dislikes:

Transportation:

History:

Goal:

Motivation:

Conflict:

Project Information

Working Title:

Genre/Subject:

Estimated Word Count:

Target Reader:

Setting:

Inciting Idea:

Blockbuster Premise:

Additional Notes

Character Information

Action Verb:

Name:

Age: Gender: Race:

Profession:

Social Class:

Strengths/Abilities:

Fears/Dislikes:

Transportation:

History:

Goal:

Motivation:

Conflict:

Synonyms for Action Verbs:

Character Information

Action Verb:

Name:

Synonyms for Action Verbs:

Age: Gender: Race:

Profession:

Social Class:

Strengths/Abilities:

Fears/Dislikes:

Transportation:

History:

Goal:

Motivation:

Conflict:

Project Information

Working Title:

Genre/Subject:

Estimated Word Count:

Target Reader:

Setting:

Inciting Idea:

Blockbuster Premise:

Additional Notes

Character Information

Action Verb:

Name:

Age: Gender: Race:

Profession:

Social Class:

Strengths/Abilities:

Fears/Dislikes:

Transportation:

History:

Goal:

Motivation:

Conflict:

Synonyms for Action Verbs:

Character Information

Action Verb:

Name:

Synonyms for Action Verbs:

Age: Gender: Race:

Profession:

Social Class:

Strengths/Abilities:

Fears/Dislikes:

Transportation:

History:

Goal:

Motivation:

Conflict:

Project Information

Working Title:

Genre/Subject:

Estimated Word Count:

Target Reader:

Setting:

Inciting Idea:

Blockbuster Premise:

Additional Notes

Character Information

Action Verb:

Name:

Synonyms for

Age: Gender: Race:

Action Verbs:

Profession:

Social Class:

Strengths/Abilities:

Fears/Dislikes:

Transportation:

History:

Goal:

Motivation:

Conflict:

Character Information

Action Verb:

Name:

Synonyms for Action Verbs:

Age: Gender: Race:

Profession:

Social Class:

Strengths/Abilities:

Fears/Dislikes:

Transportation:

History:

Goal:

Motivation:

Conflict:

Project Information

Working Title:

Genre/Subject:

Estimated Word Count:

Target Reader:

Setting:

Inciting Idea:

Blockbuster Premise:

Additional Notes

Character Information

Action Verb:

Name:

Synonyms for Action Verbs:

Age: Gender: Race:

Profession:

Social Class:

Strengths/Abilities:

Fears/Dislikes:

Transportation:

History:

Goal:

Motivation:

Conflict:

Character Information

Action Verb:

Name:

Age: Gender: Race:

Profession:

Social Class:

Strengths/Abilities:

Fears/Dislikes:

Transportation:

History:

Goal:

Motivation:

Conflict:

Synonyms for Action Verbs:

Project Information

Working Title:

Genre/Subject:

Estimated Word Count:

Target Reader:

Setting:

Inciting Idea:

Blockbuster Premise:

Additional Notes

Character Information

Action Verb:

Name:

Synonyms for Action Verbs:

Age: Gender: Race:

Profession:

Social Class:

Strengths/Abilities:

Fears/Dislikes:

Transportation:

History:

Goal:

Motivation:

Conflict:

Character Information

Action Verb:

Name:

Synonyms for Action Verbs:

Age: Gender: Race:

Profession:

Social Class:

Strengths/Abilities:

Fears/Dislikes:

Transportation:

History:

Goal:

Motivation:

Conflict:

Project Information

Working Title:

Genre/Subject:

Estimated Word Count:

Target Reader:

Setting:

Inciting Idea:

Blockbuster Premise:

Additional Notes

Character Information

Action Verb:

Name:

Age: Gender: Race:

Profession:

Social Class:

Strengths/Abilities:

Fears/Dislikes:

Transportation:

History:

Goal:

Motivation:

Conflict:

Synonyms for Action Verbs:

Character Information

Action Verb:

Name:

Synonyms for Action Verbs:

Age: Gender: Race:

Profession:

Social Class:

Strengths/Abilities:

Fears/Dislikes:

Transportation:

History:

Goal:

Motivation:

Conflict:

Project Information

Working Title:

Genre/Subject:

Estimated Word Count:

Target Reader:

Setting:

Inciting Idea:

Blockbuster Premise:

Additional Notes

Character Information

Action Verb:

Name:

Synonyms for Action Verbs:

Age: Gender: Race:

Profession:

Social Class:

Strengths/Abilities:

Fears/Dislikes:

Transportation:

History:

Goal:

Motivation:

Conflict:

Character Information

Action Verb:

Name:

Synonyms for Action Verbs:

Age: Gender: Race:

Profession:

Social Class:

Strengths/Abilities:

Fears/Dislikes:

Transportation:

History:

Goal:

Motivation:

Conflict:

Project Information

Working Title:

Genre/Subject:

Estimated Word Count:

Target Reader:

Setting:

Inciting Idea:

Blockbuster Premise:

Additional Notes

Character Information

Action Verb:

Name:

Age: Gender: Race:

Profession:

Social Class:

Strengths/Abilities:

Fears/Dislikes:

Transportation:

Synonyms for Action Verbs:

History:

Goal:

Motivation:

Conflict:

Character Information

Action Verb:

Name:

Synonyms for Action Verbs:

Age: Gender: Race:

Profession:

Social Class:

Strengths/Abilities:

Fears/Dislikes:

Transportation:

History:

Goal:

Motivation:

Conflict:

Project Information

Working Title:

Genre/Subject:

Estimated Word Count:

Target Reader:

Setting:

Inciting Idea:

Blockbuster Premise:

Additional Notes

Character Information

Action Verb:

Name:

Synonyms for Action Verbs:

Age: Gender: Race:

Profession:

Social Class:

Strengths/Abilities:

Fears/Dislikes:

Transportation:

History:

Goal:

Motivation:

Conflict:

Character Information

Action Verb:

Name:

Age: Gender: Race:

Profession:

Social Class:

Strengths/Abilities:

Fears/Dislikes:

Transportation:

Synonyms for Action Verbs:

History:

Goal:

Motivation:

Conflict:

Project Information

Working Title:

Genre/Subject:

Estimated Word Count:

Target Reader:

Setting:

Inciting Idea:

Blockbuster Premise:

Additional Notes

Character Information

Action Verb:

Name:

Synonyms for

Age: Gender: Race:

Action Verbs:

Profession:

Social Class:

Strengths/Abilities:

Fears/Dislikes:

Transportation:

History:

Goal:

Motivation:

Conflict:

Character Information

Action Verb:

Name:

Synonyms for Action Verbs:

Age: Gender: Race:

Profession:

Social Class:

Strengths/Abilities:

Fears/Dislikes:

Transportation:

History:

Goal:

Motivation:

Conflict:

Project Information

Working Title:

Genre/Subject:

Estimated Word Count:

Target Reader:

Setting:

Inciting Idea:

Blockbuster Premise:

Additional Notes

Character Information

Action Verb:

Name:

Synonyms for Action Verbs:

Age: Gender: Race:

Profession:

Social Class:

Strengths/Abilities:

Fears/Dislikes:

Transportation:

History:

Goal:

Motivation:

Conflict:

Character Information

Action Verb:

Name:

Synonyms for Action Verbs:

Age: Gender: Race:

Profession:

Social Class:

Strengths/Abilities:

Fears/Dislikes:

Transportation:

History:

Goal:

Motivation:

Conflict:

Project Information

Working Title:

Genre/Subject:

Estimated Word Count:

Target Reader:

Setting:

Inciting Idea:

Blockbuster Premise:

Additional Notes

Character Information

Action Verb:

Name:

Synonyms for Action Verbs:

Age: Gender: Race:

Profession:

Social Class:

Strengths/Abilities:

Fears/Dislikes:

Transportation:

History:

Goal:

Motivation:

Conflict:

Character Information

Action Verb:

Name:

Age: Gender: Race:

Profession:

Social Class:

Strengths/Abilities:

Fears/Dislikes:

Transportation:

Synonyms for Action Verbs:

History:

Goal:

Motivation:

Conflict:

Project Information

Working Title:

Genre/Subject:

Estimated Word Count:

Target Reader:

Setting:

Inciting Idea:

Blockbuster Premise:

Additional Notes

Character Information

Action Verb:

Name:

Age: Gender: Race:

Profession:

Social Class:

Strengths/Abilities:

Fears/Dislikes:

Transportation:

History:

Goal:

Motivation:

Conflict:

Synonyms for Action Verbs:

Character Information

Action Verb:

Name:

Synonyms for Action Verbs:

Age: Gender: Race:

Profession:

Social Class:

Strengths/Abilities:

Fears/Dislikes:

Transportation:

History:

Goal:

Motivation:

Conflict:

Project Information

Working Title:

Genre/Subject:

Estimated Word Count:

Target Reader:

Setting:

Inciting Idea:

Blockbuster Premise:

Additional Notes

Character Information

Action Verb:

Name:

Synonyms for

Age: Gender: Race:

Action Verbs:

Profession:

Social Class:

Strengths/Abilities:

Fears/Dislikes:

Transportation:

History:

Goal:

Motivation:

Conflict:

Character Information

Action Verb:

Name:

Synonyms for Action Verbs:

Age: Gender: Race:

Profession:

Social Class:

Strengths/Abilities:

Fears/Dislikes:

Transportation:

History:

Goal:

Motivation:

Conflict:

Project Information

Working Title:

Genre/Subject:

Estimated Word Count:

Target Reader:

Setting:

Inciting Idea:

Blockbuster Premise:

Additional Notes

Character Information

Action Verb:

Name:

Age: Gender: Race:

Profession:

Social Class:

Strengths/Abilities:

Fears/Dislikes:

Transportation:

History:

Goal:

Motivation:

Conflict:

Synonyms for Action Verbs:

Character Information

Action Verb:

Name:

Synonyms for Action Verbs:

Age: Gender: Race:

Profession:

Social Class:

Strengths/Abilities:

Fears/Dislikes:

Transportation:

History:

Goal:

Motivation:

Conflict:

Project Information

Working Title:

Genre/Subject:

Estimated Word Count:

Target Reader:

Setting:

Inciting Idea:

Blockbuster Premise:

Additional Notes

Character Information

Action Verb:

Name:

Synonyms for Action Verbs:

Age: Gender: Race:

Profession:

Social Class:

Strengths/Abilities:

Fears/Dislikes:

Transportation:

History:

Goal:

Motivation:

Conflict:

Character Information

Action Verb:

Name:

Age: Gender: Race:

Profession:

Social Class:

Strengths/Abilities:

Fears/Dislikes:

Transportation:

History:

Goal:

Motivation:

Conflict:

Synonyms for Action Verbs:

Project Information

Working Title:

Genre/Subject:

Estimated Word Count:

Target Reader:

Setting:

Inciting Idea:

Blockbuster Premise:

Additional Notes

Character Information

Action Verb:

Name:

Synonyms for Action Verbs:

Age: Gender: Race:

Profession:

Social Class:

Strengths/Abilities:

Fears/Dislikes:

Transportation:

History:

Goal:

Motivation:

Conflict:

Character Information

Action Verb:

Name:

Age: Gender: Race:

Profession:

Social Class:

Strengths/Abilities:

Fears/Dislikes:

Transportation:

History:

Goal:

Motivation:

Conflict:

Synonyms for Action Verbs:

Project Information

Working Title:

Genre/Subject:

Estimated Word Count:

Target Reader:

Setting:

Inciting Idea:

Blockbuster Premise:

Additional Notes

Character Information

Action Verb:

Name:

Synonyms for Action Verbs:

Age: Gender: Race:

Profession:

Social Class:

Strengths/Abilities:

Fears/Dislikes:

Transportation:

History:

Goal:

Motivation:

Conflict:

Character Information

Action Verb:

Name:

Age: Gender: Race:

Profession:

Social Class:

Strengths/Abilities:

Fears/Dislikes:

Transportation:

History:

Goal:

Motivation:

Conflict:

Synonyms for Action Verbs:

Project Information

Working Title:

Genre/Subject:

Estimated Word Count:

Target Reader:

Setting:

Inciting Idea:

Blockbuster Premise:

Additional Notes

Character Information

Action Verb:

Name:

Synonyms for Action Verbs:

Age: Gender: Race:

Profession:

Social Class:

Strengths/Abilities:

Fears/Dislikes:

Transportation:

History:

Goal:

Motivation:

Conflict:

Character Information

Action Verb:

Name:

Synonyms for Action Verbs:

Age: Gender: Race:

Profession:

Social Class:

Strengths/Abilities:

Fears/Dislikes:

Transportation:

History:

Goal:

Motivation:

Conflict:

Project Information

Working Title:

Genre/Subject:

Estimated Word Count:

Target Reader:

Setting:

Inciting Idea:

Blockbuster Premise:

Additional Notes

Character Information

Action Verb:

Name:

Age: Gender: Race:

Profession:

Social Class:

Strengths/Abilities:

Fears/Dislikes:

Transportation:

History:

Goal:

Motivation:

Conflict:

Synonyms for Action Verbs:

Character Information

Action Verb:

Name:

Age: Gender: Race:

Profession:

Social Class:

Strengths/Abilities:

Fears/Dislikes:

Transportation:

History:

Goal:

Motivation:

Conflict:

Synonyms for Action Verbs:

Project Information

Working Title:

Genre/Subject:

Estimated Word Count:

Target Reader:

Setting:

Inciting Idea:

Blockbuster Premise:

Additional Notes

Character Information

Action Verb:

Name:

Synonyms for Action Verbs:

Age: Gender: Race:

Profession:

Social Class:

Strengths/Abilities:

Fears/Dislikes:

Transportation:

History:

Goal:

Motivation:

Conflict:

Character Information

Action Verb:

Name:

Synonyms for Action Verbs:

Age: Gender: Race:

Profession:

Social Class:

Strengths/Abilities:

Fears/Dislikes:

Transportation:

History:

Goal:

Motivation:

Conflict:

Project Information

Working Title:

Genre/Subject:

Estimated Word Count:

Target Reader:

Setting:

Inciting Idea:

Blockbuster Premise:

Additional Notes

Character Information

Action Verb:

Name:

Synonyms for

Age: Gender: Race:

Action Verbs:

Profession:

Social Class:

Strengths/Abilities:

Fears/Dislikes:

Transportation:

History:

Goal:

Motivation:

Conflict:

Character Information

Action Verb:

Name:

Synonyms for Action Verbs:

Age: Gender: Race:

Profession:

Social Class:

Strengths/Abilities:

Fears/Dislikes:

Transportation:

History:

Goal:

Motivation:

Conflict:

Project Information

Working Title:

Genre/Subject:

Estimated Word Count:

Target Reader:

Setting:

Inciting Idea:

Blockbuster Premise:

Additional Notes

Character Information

Action Verb:

Name:

Synonyms for Action Verbs:

Age: Gender: Race:

Profession:

Social Class:

Strengths/Abilities:

Fears/Dislikes:

Transportation:

History:

Goal:

Motivation:

Conflict:

Character Information

Action Verb:

Name:

Age: Gender: Race:

Profession:

Social Class:

Strengths/Abilities:

Fears/Dislikes:

Transportation:

Synonyms for Action Verbs:

History:

Goal:

Motivation:

Conflict:

Project Information

Working Title:

Genre/Subject:

Estimated Word Count:

Target Reader:

Setting:

Inciting Idea:

Blockbuster Premise:

Additional Notes

Character Information

Action Verb:

Name:

Synonyms for Action Verbs:

Age: Gender: Race:

Profession:

Social Class:

Strengths/Abilities:

Fears/Dislikes:

Transportation:

History:

Goal:

Motivation:

Conflict:

Character Information

Action Verb: ....

Name: ....

Synonyms for Action Verbs:

....

....

....

....

....

....

....

Age: .... Gender: .... Race: ....

Profession: ....

Social Class: ....

Strengths/Abilities: ....

....

Fears/Dislikes: ....

....

Transportation: ....

History: ....

....

....

Goal: ....

....

....

Motivation: ....

....

....

Conflict: ....

....

....

Project Information

Working Title:

Genre/Subject:

Estimated Word Count:

Target Reader:

Setting:

Inciting Idea:

Blockbuster Premise:

Additional Notes

Character Information

Action Verb:

Name:

Synonyms for Action Verbs:

Age: Gender: Race:

Profession:

Social Class:

Strengths/Abilities:

Fears/Dislikes:

Transportation:

History:

Goal:

Motivation:

Conflict:

Character Information

Action Verb:

Name:

Age: Gender: Race:

Profession:

Social Class:

Strengths/Abilities:

Fears/Dislikes:

Transportation:

History:

Goal:

Motivation:

Conflict:

Synonyms for Action Verbs:

If you're having trouble coming up with ideas, below are a few resources to help.

Creative Play: A Guide for the Artistic Path by award winning author Michele Venné, gives writers proven techniques for tapping into their creative side.

Be sure to have a copy of Damon Suede's *Verbalize* on hand to create true-to-life compelling characters and learn how to keep your story coherent. He also explains how the action verbs work in character development.

A couple of must-haves for your library are Julie Cameron's *The Artist's Way* and Stephen Pressfield's *The War of Art.*

Plus, Anatomy of Story: 72 Steps to Becoming a Master Storyteller by John Truby, *No Plot? No Problem by* Chris Baty, and *The Writer's Journey* by Christopher Vogler are all super helpful.

Another great reference for creativity is, *What If? Writing Exercises for Fiction Writers* by Anne Bernays and Pamela Painter.

Also, go to *The Story Starter* at:

http://thestorystarter.com/ and check out their story idea generator.

Visit the *Creativity Portal* for prompts and hundreds of unique ideas for stories and other creative projects. http://creativity-portal.com/

Never fear the blank page again when you click on either Tumbler or Reddit for more writing prompts and inspiration than you can possibly handle:

http://writingprompts.tumblr.com/ and

https://reddit.com/r/WritingPrompts/

Try a bit of advice from successful authors on how they become (and stay) inspired to put pen to page. https://thejohnfox.com/2016/06/writing-inspiration/

Join a writing group such as Romance Writers of America, Sisters in Crime, or the Society of Children's Book Writers and Illustrators. Even if you don't write in those genres, these clubs often have fundamental information for writers at each level of the profession.

If nothing else works, pick up a book, copy the first sentence, and then begin to write your own story from there.

In my experience, the best way to write is to sit your butt down and write. Have fun with it!

Other Books and Projects by Anna Questerly Available Online & in Bookstores

A couple of resources for writers!

The Minstrel's Tale Trilogy

A fun, family read, filled with original fairy tales that the minstrel tells while he's on his own adventure in 14th century Europe.

Individual fairy tales from The Minstrel's Tale!

A reference guide for those new to essential oils, written as The Alchemist's Guild

91664140R00117

Made in the USA
San Bernardino, CA
31 October 2018